CANADA'S
MOUNTAIN
ANIMALS

Chelsea Donaldson

Scholastic Canada Ltd.

Toronto New York London Auckland Sydney
Mexico City New Delhi Hong Kong Buenos Aires

Scholastic Canada Ltd.
604 King Street West, Toronto, Ontario M5V 1E1, Canada

Scholastic Inc.
557 Broadway, New York, NY 10012, USA

Scholastic Australia Pty Limited
PO Box 579, Gosford, NSW 2250, Australia

Scholastic New Zealand Limited
Private Bag 94407, Greenmount, Auckland, New Zealand

Scholastic Children's Books
Euston House, 24 Eversholt Street, London NW1 1DB, UK

Every reasonable effort has been made to trace the ownership of copyright material used in the text. The publisher would be pleased to know of any errors or omissions.

Visual Credits
Front cover: © Alan & Sandy Carey/Ivy Images; pp. i (centre), 2, 5, 12, 13, 14–15, 16, 18, 20–21, 25, 26, 30, 31, 33, 43, 44 (centre): © Tom & Pat Leeson; i & iii (border): © iStockphoto.com/Randy Mayes; iv (map) © HotHouse Design Studio; iv–1 (mountains): © Alan Fortune/Animals Animals–Earth Scenes/Maxx Images Inc.; p. 3: © Bret Edge/age fotostock/Maxx Images Inc.; p. 4: © SuperStock/Maxx Images Inc.; p. 6: © Ken McGraw/Index Stock/Maxx Images Inc.; pp. 7, 8, 17, 19, 23, 28, 34, 35: © Thomas Kitchin & Victoria Hurst; pp. 9, 27: © Alan & Sandy Carey/ Ivy Images; pp. 10–11: © Eric Baccega/age fotostock/Maxx Images Inc.; p. 22: © Jim Brandenburg/ Minden Pictures; pp. 24, 42: © Ralph Reinhold/Animals Animals–Earth Scenes/Maxx Images Inc.; p. 29: © Paul Higgins; p. 36: © W. Lankinen/Ivy Images; p. 37: © Len Lee Rue Jr./Ivy Images; p. 38: © Daniel J. Cox/Naturalexposures.com; p. 39: © Wayne Lankinen/DRK Phot; p. 40: © SCPhotos/Alamy; p. 41: © Barbara Von Hoffmann/Animals Animals–Earth Scenes/Maxx Images Inc.; p. 44 (left): © iStockphoto.com/Stefan Ekernas; p. 44 (right): Photodisc via SODA; back cover: © iStockphoto.com/Len Tillim

Developed and Produced by Focus Strategic Communications Inc.
Project Management and Editorial: Adrianna Edwards
Design and Layout: Lisa Platt
Photo Research: Elizabeth Kelly

Special thanks to Dr. Bill Freedman of Dalhousie University for his expertise.

Library and Archives Canada Cataloguing in Publication
Donaldson, Chelsea, 1959-
Canada's mountain animals / Chelsea Donaldson.
(Canada close up)
ISBN 978-0-545-99487-3
1. Mountain animals--Canada--Juvenile literature.
I. Title. II. Series: Canada close up (Toronto, Ont.)
QL113.D65 2008   j591.75'30971   C2007-907183-X

ISBN-10: 0-545-99487-X

Copyright © 2008 by Scholastic Canada Ltd.

6 5 4 3 2 1   Printed in Canada   08 09 10 11 12

TABLE OF CONTENTS

Canada's Mountains

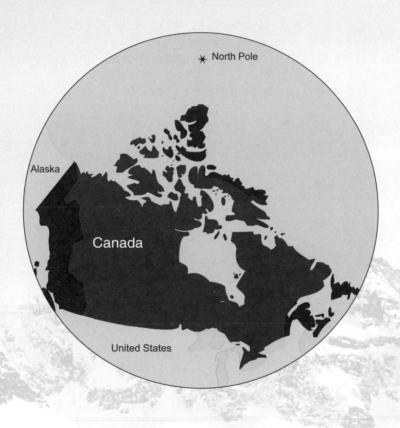

North Pole

Alaska

Canada

United States

Canada's Main Mountain Ranges

Canada

United States

Welcome to the Mountains!

In Canada, we have three main mountain ranges: the Appalachians, the Western cordillera (cor-dee-AIR-ah) and the Arctic cordillera. A mountain range is a group of mountains.

The oldest mountains in Canada are the Appalachians, on the eastern side of the country. These mountains are about 250 million years old! The biggest and highest mountain range, along the west coast, is called the Western cordillera. It includes the Rocky Mountains. The Arctic cordillera is in the Far North. This is the most northerly mountain range in the world. It is so cold that few plants and animals can live there.

Canada's mountain ranges are home to some fascinating animals. Let's climb up and get a better view!

CHAPTER ONE

Mountain Goat

Mountain goats have hoofs and horns like other goats, but they are not directly related to goats. Their shaggy coats make them look a bit like sheep. But they aren't related to sheep, either.

In fact, mountain goats are not closely related to any other animal in North America. They are one-of-a-kind creatures. For hundreds of thousands of years, they have lived high up in the mountains. They are perfectly built for life on the slopes.

Not many animals can climb as well as mountain goats. Their hoofs have special foot pads that act like suction cups to help grip slippery rocks. The hoofs are also cloven, or split into two toes in a V shape. This way, mountain goats can jam them into rocks when going downhill.

Mountain goats' legs are short and close together, so they can perch on ledges only a few centimetres wide. They can even turn around on a narrow ledge without falling, and jump across gaps up to three metres wide. Their huge shoulders and chest muscles help them power up hills.

The female goat, or nanny, usually gives birth to one baby at a time. The baby goat is called a kid. (Male goats are called billies.) The kid is often born on a ledge high up on a mountain where predators such as grizzly bears and coyotes cannot go. But the nanny still has to watch out for eagles. They sometimes try to knock the kid off the ledge.

When it is just a few hours old, the kid starts to climb. Within a few days, it can follow its mother almost anywhere.

During the summer, mountain goats stay high up in the mountain. They graze on shrubs and grasses.

As it gets colder, food becomes harder to find. The goats may then move down the mountain a bit or find a steep slope where the snow cover won't stick. That way, they can get to food that would otherwise be buried. Even so, during winters with heavy snowfall, young mountain goats may starve.

While finding enough food may be a problem for mountain goats, keeping warm isn't. Mountain goats have two layers of fur. The bottom layer is thick and woolly like a warm sweater. The top layer acts like a raincoat. It has longer hairs, called guard hairs, that protect the animal from wind, rain, snow and sleet.

When spring comes, mountain goats shed their winter coat in clumps. They can look very ragged for a while. Now that's what you call a bad hair day!

CHAPTER TWO

Grizzly Bear

One of the easiest ways to tell a grizzly
bear apart from its smaller cousin,
the black bear, is by its shoulder hump.
Grizzly bears, or brown bears, are bigger
than black bears. They can grow up to
three metres long. When a grizzly bear
stands up on its hind legs, it is taller than
any human! Grizzly bears have long claws
and flat, round faces that look a bit like a
dish. But don't get too close to a grizzly
bear. These bears are very fierce!

Plants, vegetables, fruit and small insects make up most of a grizzly bear's diet. But they will also kill and eat elk, deer, caribou and fish.

Grizzly bears love berries. In the fall, a single grizzly bear can eat as many as 50,000 berries in one day. That's a lot of berries!

Grizzly bears eat a lot in the fall because they have to prepare for the long winter months. Like other bears, grizzlies hibernate (HI-bur-nate). This means they sleep for most of the winter.

A grizzly starts getting ready for hibernation in November. If it can't find a comfy rock cave or hollow tree, the bear may dig its own den. The den has a tunnel that slopes downward underground. Then the grizzly bear crawls inside, yawns and settles down for a long and deep sleep.

While the grizzly sleeps, snow covers the entrance to its den. The snow acts like a big blanket, keeping the space inside warm until spring.

A female grizzly gives birth inside her den during the winter. Usually there are two tiny cubs. They stay close beside their mother — sleeping, drinking her milk and growing bigger day by day.

In April or May, the cubs come out of the den for the first time. They are very playful — running, sliding, jumping and tumbling as their mother looks for food. Their mother shows them where to dig for roots, where the first fresh green shoots will come up and how to stay out of trouble.

Over the months that follow, the family sticks closely together. The cubs stay with their mother for two to four years. Then they go off on their own.

Bye, Mom!

CHAPTER THREE

Bighorn Sheep

Bighorn sheep get their name from their most noticeable feature — their amazing horns. In males, or rams, the horns curl back from their foreheads and then spiral forward around their ears. Females, or ewes, have much shorter horns.

You can also recognize them by their rear ends. It looks like they sat in a bucket of white paint! Thank goodness no one thought to name them after *that* feature!

Each spring, pregnant ewes go off to give birth on their own. Lambs learn to walk within a few hours after being born and can follow their mothers back to the flock in a few days.

The lambs amuse themselves by playing together. Their games look a lot like games you might play — such as King of the Castle and Follow the Leader!

The mating season for bighorn sheep is in November. Rams gather and size up their competition. Suddenly, they rear up on their hind legs and run at each other. When they meet, they bang their foreheads together. *THUD. THUD. THUD.*

It's hard to believe that all that hitting doesn't hurt the rams. Luckily, they have extra-thick bony plates on their foreheads to help them absorb the blows. They usually suffer nothing worse than a chipped horn — and perhaps a bad headache!

The battle can go on for hours. The rams attack each other over and over, sometimes one on one, sometimes two on one. Then, as suddenly as it began, the contest is over.

To human eyes, it's hard to figure out who won. But the rams know, and so do the ewes. The other males back off and allow the winner first chance to mate.

CHAPTER FOUR

Cougar

Cougars, also called mountain lions, can survive in all sorts of habitats. They were once found across southern Canada — as far east as New Brunswick and Nova Scotia. Then people began to take over many of the areas where cougars lived. Today, only a few eastern cougars exist. Cougars are more plentiful in the west, especially in mountainous areas away from humans. The mountains give them places to hide and food to eat.

Cougars are not quite as big as their larger cousins: lions, tigers and leopards. And they don't roar. Instead, they snarl, hiss, whistle, scream and purrrrrrrrr!

Cougars are fast runners and good jumpers. They can leap up to six metres onto a tree branch. That would be like you jumping onto the rim of a basketball net!

A female cougar gives birth to as many as six kittens at a time. For the first week or so, the kittens are tiny, fluffy and blind. They live off their mother's milk for the first three months, until their mother starts to bring them solid food.

The young cougars stay with their mother for the first year or two. During that time, they learn to hunt by sneaking up on their prey and biting the back of its neck. Their long, sharp teeth and strong neck muscles are perfect for clamping down and holding on.

Cougars eat small creatures such as pikas, mice, beavers and rabbits. But they prefer bigger prey such as deer, moose and elk.

Cougars usually stay well away from humans. Occasionally, though, a cougar may attack a human who comes too close.

CHAPTER FIVE

Elk

A male elk spends most of the summer eating as much as it can to build up its strength. Then in the fall, it uses every ounce of its energy to attract females to its harem.

It is a lot of work. The male, or bull, has to be constantly on its guard, fending off other bulls who want to steal its females, or cows. The more cows it attracts, the harder it becomes for the male to keep rivals away.

A cow chooses a bull to breed with partly by its mating call — the louder and stronger, the better. The call is known as a bugle, but it sounds more like a very loud, high whistle. It can be heard from several kilometres away.

Antlers also play a role in attracting a cow. A bull's antlers can grow to almost two metres wide. (A female does not have antlers.) The antlers get so heavy, a bull has special neck muscles just to hold them up. A bull with broken or missing antlers has no chance of attracting a harem. But a bull with a strong bugle and big antlers may gather up to 20 cows to mate with.

Once the mating season is over, the males wander off alone or in small groups to rest and regain their strength. Over the winter, they shed their antlers and begin to grow a new pair.

The cows and older calves stick together in large herds for safety during the winter. In the spring, pregnant cows leave the herd to give birth alone. Mothers keep their newborn calves hidden in tall grass for about two weeks.

Those two weeks are the most dangerous time in a young elk's life. The mother hovers nearby, keeping a careful eye out for coyotes, bears and other predators. If she senses danger, she gives a special call. The call tells the calf to crouch down and be very quiet until the danger has passed.

Calves have no scent, making it harder for predators to find them. Even so, many calves are killed by predators in their first two weeks of life. Those that survive rejoin the safety of the herd.

CHAPTER SIX

Hoary Marmot

A ground squirrel the size of a cat? Believe it or not, that's a pretty good description of a hoary marmot. The marmot is the largest member of the North American squirrel family.

Marmots have a lot of fat, and loose furry coats that allow them to live in cold temperatures high up in the mountains. In fact, you can find these charming creatures as far north as the southern Yukon and Northwest Territories.

Hoary marmots spend a large part of their lives hibernating. During hibernation, their breathing and heart rates slow down, and they do not have to eat to stay alive. When they are not hibernating, marmots like to lie on warm rocks in the sun. The rest of their time is spent feeding — and playing.

Marmot play looks a lot like wrestling. Two marmots stand on their hind legs, face each other and grab each other's fur. Then the battle is on! It ends quickly, though, if either of them lets out a yelp.

Marmots like to play, but they are always on guard against predators. Their main enemies include lynx, golden eagles, foxes, coyotes, bears and wolverines.

With so many predators to worry about, marmots have come up with a clever defence system. At the first sign of danger, a lookout marmot gives a shrill whistle. Other marmots can tell from the sound of the whistle what type of predator is approaching and how close it is. Then, they all run for their burrows.

Hoary marmots live in colonies. A colony usually includes one male, several females and the young from the previous year. When the young males are old enough to survive on their own, the older male chases them away. They have to find a new place to live. About half of the young females are chased out as well.

Marmots rarely intrude on the territory of other marmots. They stay in their family groups — eating, sleeping and playing — until it is time for another long winter hibernation.

CHAPTER SEVEN

Harlequin Duck

The icy water of a mountain river tumbles and churns. Building speed, it crashes against rocks on its way down to the sea.

But wait, what's that, bobbing on the surface of the river? It's a small bird about the size of a pigeon. And it doesn't seem to mind the rushing water at all. In fact, it's bobbing in the foam like a cork!

Meet the harlequin duck.

A harlequin duck is smaller than most other ducks. A full-grown adult is no bigger than a small loaf of bread. The female is light brown with three round white spots on its face. The male, though, is very colourful. It looks a bit like a clown, with its patchwork of red, blue, white and black.

In fact, that is where the harlequin duck gets its name. Harlequin is the name of a clown in Italian folk tales. He wore a brightly coloured suit and had a painted face.

Harlequin ducks spend their time
swimming in rough waters. The rougher,
the better! They spend their summers
beside fast-flowing mountain rivers in
both eastern and western Canada.
In winter, they migrate to the coasts.

You might expect animals that live so close
to water to feed on fish. But harlequin
ducks prefer the larvae of insects such as
blackflies and midges, as well as crabs,
fish eggs and small molluscs. Harlequins
dive to the bottom of a stream or river.
Then they swim along the bottom, flipping
over stones to find their favourite food.

Harlequin ducks are born in a nest on a shore near fast-flowing water. The female lays three to eight eggs and sits on them for about 28 days. When the eggs hatch, the mother leads her ducklings to water. She takes them on their first swim and teaches them how to find food.

The ducklings have no problem swimming — they know how to do it from the moment they are born. But it takes them about 40 to 50 days to learn how to fly. When the time is right, they take off into the skies, swooping and gliding alongside their mother.

CHAPTER EIGHT

Pika

Pikas are smaller relatives of rabbits and hares. They have round ears, no tail, and an egg-shaped body. Full-grown pikas are about the size of guinea pigs. They look a lot like mice.

Pikas live in the mountains because that is where they are most likely to find their favourite habitat: a pile of rocks next to a meadow. The rocks give them shelter from eagles and other predators. The meadow has grasses and flowers that they like to eat.

In the mountains the weather stays cool, even in summer, which also suits pikas. Pikas are common in the southern Yukon, Northwest Territories and British Columbia.

Pikas spend much of the summer gathering flowers and grasses from the meadow. They spread the plants out on the rocks to dry before storing them in a big "haystack" in their den.

Some of the plants pikas choose are actually a bit poisonous. But pikas know that the poison helps keep the plants fresh longer and that the poison will disappear over time. By including a variety of plants in their haystack, pikas make sure they will have healthy food all through the winter.

Many pikas may share the same rock pile, but they don't spend much time together. Instead, each animal has its own territory. If one pika sees another one coming too close, it will chase the intruder away.

But when they are frightened, pikas have a special call to warn their neighbours of danger. Their call seems to come from several different places at once. This confuses predators and makes pikas harder to catch.

Pikas mate in the spring. As many as six babies are born to a female. The mother cares for them in her nest in the rock pile. The babies begin to eat solid food in about three weeks, just as the first, nutritious shoots start to appear in the meadow. Not long after, the young pikas leave to find their own territories.

Soon, they will be hard at work, building their own haystacks.

CHAPTER NINE

Ermine

No matter where you go in Canada, there are probably ermine living nearby. These long, slim weasels are found in every province and territory. They live high up in the mountains as well as down in the valleys and plains.

In summer, an ermine has a light brown coat. But when the snow comes, it turns pure white to blend in with its snowy surroundings.

Well, almost pure white. The tip of its tail stays black, making it easy to spot against the white snow. This fools owls and other birds that might try to catch the ermine as food. They attack the wrong end of the ermine! With luck, this gives the ermine time to skitter away to safety.

Ermine build nests in tangles of tree roots, hollow logs and piles of rocks. They also take over abandoned burrows of other animals. They line the burrow with fur to make it as warm as possible for the winter. Sometimes, ermine will store food in their burrows to see them through times when food is scarce.

Females give birth to about six babies in spring. Each baby weighs only about as much as a penny. The babies' eyes are shut tight, and they have no fur. They huddle close to their mother for safety and warmth.

In a few months, the babies have grown their brown summer coats, their eyes are open, and they start to play outside the burrow. Their mother brings them live voles and mice so they can practise hunting. This is great fun for the young ermine — but not so much fun for the mice!

Adult ermine are excellent hunters. Quick
as lightning and very fierce, they leap on
their prey and kill it with a single bite.
Ermine eat mostly small creatures like
mice, but they also can take on larger
prey such as pikas, red squirrels, young
hares and even birds.

In snowy areas, it's easy to tell if an
ermine has been around. Just look for
tracks that ZIG one way, ZAG another
— and then turn back upon themselves.
Ermine hardly ever walk in a straight line!

CHAPTER TEN

Golden Eagle

Up in the mountains, a golden eagle soars high overhead, riding the currents of warmed air that rise over the mountain peaks. Its long, powerful wings beat only when necessary as it turns in big circles looking for prey.

But don't be fooled by its lazy circles. A golden eagle can fly up to 100 kilometres an hour, and twice that fast when it swoops down to capture its prey. It's no wonder the golden eagle is one of the most feared mountain predators.

Being able to fly is a big advantage in the mountains. It makes it possible to see over long distances. It also makes it easier to travel without worrying about rocky ground, landslides or slippery slopes.

Of course, if you want to be able to find small prey from the air, you need to have good eyesight. And like all birds of prey, golden eagles have excellent vision. They can see a rabbit hopping across a mountain meadow from as far away as three kilometres!

Golden eagles do not turn a golden colour until they are four or five years old. That is when their neck feathers turn a lovely golden brown. Before that, they are plain brown with white patches. Once fully grown, golden eagles are the largest birds of prey in Canada. When their wings are spread out in flight, they are HUGE!

Unlike other eagles, golden eagles have feathers all the way down to their toes, kind of like trousers. Their claws are strong enough to pick up and carry a weight up to three kilograms.

Most of a golden eagle's diet is made up of rabbits, hares, marmots and ground squirrels. It can also attack large birds like geese while they are in the air.
A golden eagle is so strong, it has even been known to take down a small deer!

Sometimes eagles hunt in pairs.
One chases down the prey to tire it out, while the second swoops in for the kill.
More often, though, they are lone hunters.

Look up in the sky! It's a bird. It's a plane. It's Superman. No wait . . . it *is* a bird!

Mountains are among the last places where animals can go and not be disturbed by humans. The rocks, valleys, streams and forested slopes provide them with plenty of hiding places.

Surefooted climbers . . .
expert swimmers . . .
and high flyers . . .

Canada's mountain animals are magnificent!